EVERYTHING
and Other Poems

Charles North

The Song Cave

The Song Cave
www.the-song-cave.com

Cover image: by Pieter Bruegel the Elder, *The Battle Between Carnival and Lent, 1559* (detail)

Design and layout by Janet Evans-Scanlon

ISBN: 978-1-7340351-0-0
Library of Congress Control Number: 2019953294

FIRST EDITION

Contents

Pain Quotient

for David Watson

1

How to explain tragedy to a deer. This is the assignment.—Well, it isn't the assignment it's in the general category of things assigned, like growing to a mature height of four inches if you happen to be a certain strain of ornamental cactus, or being shamed back to life by any means possible. I like the idea that hope springs eternal especially as the adjective, not adverb suggests that spring is a verb of being rather than action, it doesn't have to be imagined or looked forward to, or yearned for, or original in any sense of the word. The present which is always with us, regardless. Take the piano music of objects, the black-and-white, the mystical harmonics, bipolarities, etc.

2

The afternoon smells like rosemary, whereas the morning was on the visual side, jutting among the albums. Someone David knew, an actress, referred to the café Pain Quotidien as Pain Quotient, apparently with a straight face. *The Daily Pain* (which I seem to remember my father bringing home from work). Or if you happen to be in show business, the pan. Take the extremist willows.

3

5:30 p.m. The soul goes out for its walk—just be sure you're back in time for supper. The colors look pasted on, washy blue like a robin's egg seen through a landlord shade, then just washed away. Where is conceptual art when you need it. Everyone knows that Janus Weathercock and Cornelius Van Vinckboons are too good not to be true, but very few know of their connection to the poet John Clare. Or that "they" were in fact the same person, who not only worked for *London Magazine* in the early part of the 19th century but was, according to Clare's biographer Jonathan Bate, "the Oscar Wilde of his day." I say metaphors have it easy. Brahms surging, receding, churning the already churned foam of Being

whereas Rachmaninov is like a fist to the heart.

4

Suppose everyone were a lot less talkative. Or were prohibited from talking to anyone who spoke the same language, not only people but houseplants, raccoons, self-service elevators, winged salesmen from the future, etc. A gem-like solid framed by a ribbon of aluminum light. Begins in speech but is diverted primarily by all the mistakes from the remembered past. Another episode has a word whirling around its phonemes which are also whirling. We were talking about shaming someone back into life, the blood verities; hanging in the air "like a memory lost" but recapturable if you don't mind the mix of truth and sprawl, fragments of all that can be thought without accompaniment or fixation. Or *whatness.* Characters get dragged in kicking and screaming from the wings and forget their resonant ties to objects. To be calmer than a rug, a particle from the 1940s, dizzying, I'll take it. But you can have the stifling dream states, like a perpetual air-raid. Why so many notions settling in the middle of the forehead like a *tableau vivant*—so much more cause than affect. The summer retired early; was forced out actually like the recorder family from mainstream music. Mixed-use but heartfelt skyline.

Crepuscule with Paula

Does realism get your vote? It gets mine.
The plants with their insatiable thirst for appearances,
the heart-stopping 7:00 p.m. air moonlighting as a pressed-
    cardboard Korean ashtray
(server, modest coaster) decorated with a single blondish branch
holding six leaves and a piece of rose-colored fruit (pear,
    plum, ripe peach)
slightly raised as if applied to the flat, creamy space behind
flecked with light gray, light green, and brown marks of varying
    size
from pinpricks to ashes, pencil (it looks like) to brush.
The romance of the window panes (I'm squinting a little) has
    nothing
to do with the misguided view, the one with the Fates schmoozing
under the maroon awning of the high-rise (schmoos is more like
    it)
and the embarrassed-looking sycamores revealing for all they're
    worth
in their slightly fictionalized but emotionally accurate way,
    which contributes to the overall tone
without detracting from the realistic participation,
a motorbike taking the corner too fast, a cat knowing the worst
    that can possibly happen and managing to avoid it,
which could be the key signature if not for a free-standing
radiance just outside, unmoored, a hint of plum or Anjou pear.

What Doesn't Have an Embouchure

The duck, for one, but the voice
has to go someplace.
It looks like a sycamore factory.
Most of the areas on the map
are dragged into sleep
yet a steady glimpse into the future
empties shaded ballfields and
whatever else smacks of a dream state.
As much from the ground up
as the burnished architectural crown in mist.
Scatter the keys. The air
in the park sends its small invasions
Norman style, but that's between
you and your inner life.

French Licks

for Ron Padgett

What do you want me to say, that I saw Picasso, Gaston Leroux, Carco, Giraudoux, admirals on shore leave, the Guimet Museum, schools for everything under the sun, Aragon, Saint-Ex, Gertrude Stein, fuel oil, people doing business deals, soccer, Rainer Maria Rilke . . . everything I can possibly think of?

—LÉON-PAUL FARGUE

At one end of the bridge that squashes the water underneath it, a cop just took out his ticket book.

—MAX JACOB

Even dead I'm an insomniac!

—JULES SUPERVIELLE

O night, if only you didn't have stars
Pouring out their hackneyed phrases.
I want emptiness! Blackness! Bare nothingness!

—CHARLES BAUDELAIRE

The dog in the fireplace just woke up
The cat with the cigarette is purring in front
It doesn't look like anyone needs a drink
The wine is corked anyway

That odd hat covering your forehead
Pointed and ugly
Watch out your ideas don't leave when you take it off

—PIERRE REVERDY

. . . bread is supposed to be eaten, not only honored in a poem.

—FRANCIS PONGE

I detest working! Lazy, half asleep,
With the one hand not buried under the covers
I barely managed to write you this poem. Barely.

—MARC-ANTOINE GIRARD DE SAINT-AMANT

Did anyone see the toad cross the street? He's tiny, no bigger than a doll, going on his knees. Embarrassed? Not at all. Arthritic. He has to drag each leg ahead of him. Where to? He came up out of a sewer pipe, poor guy. Not a soul noticed. It used to be that way with me, now they mock my yellow star. Lucky toad! You don't have to drag a yellow star everywhere you go.

—MAX JACOB

A drizzle
All over Europe
Everyone's
In the same boat
Never mind the infantry
Busy with their guns
Or the scary newspaper headlines,

Constant drizzle
Making the flags go limp

—JULES SUPERVIELLE

Your eyes aren't eyes, they're gods.
They hold sway over kings.
Did I say gods? Make it blue heavens
With the same flashes and dartings.

Heavens? How about brilliant suns
Blinding us to everything else.
Suns? More like lightning bolts
That give a hint of the force of our love.

The pain I feel couldn't come from a god.
The heavens are one thing not two.
As for the sun, who doesn't know it's unique?

Sunrays? They don't hold a candle to your eyes!
Yet the false comparisons all shed light:
Eyes, gods, heavens, suns, and their brilliance.

—HONORAT LAUGIER DE PORCHÈRES

Just before the bell of night, when the seasonal canvas ruffles and the sun draws honey from the bodies of women in bed, and every ship with its vowels and its incest sets sail, solo, to the shrill flutes of Europe . . .

—SAINT-JOHN PERSE

Almost dawn and no one else around
The milkman's cans wake up the street

—GUILLAUME APOLLINAIRE

The future arrived but it's lazy.

—PAUL VALÉRY

I remember what winter coats smell like, dogs running under the table, saucers clinking while cabinet ministers fell, time's anger, pretty women's laughter strewn on the floor like turtle dove feathers, the canon of theories designed to order or else disrupt, handshakes indicating contrary states of mind, tumultuous and peaceful, puffed up, sub rosa, unnoticed yet ringing with health like a Gothic steeple.

—LÉON-PAUL FARGUE

. . . tall, svelte locomotives speeding
Effortlessly through the lonely Serbian mountains
Followed by four yellow cars with gold writing on them
And beyond, across rose-strewn Bulgaria . . .

—VALERY LARBAUD

It all comes down to Time, naturally. (For you, too?) We have to beat it at its own game if you know what I mean, beat it to the punch. You know the one about the flea inside the drawer? I'm sure you do. It makes perfect sense! I really don't know what else to say. Am I ever going to see you?

—HENRI MICHAUX

One of the star roses falls every night
A prize for the best dream

—ROBERT DESNOS

The kings never even touch the door

so how can they possibly know how it feels to push open one of these two-dimensional friendly giants, forcefully or not, or to return it to its original position. Holding it in one's arms.

—FRANCIS PONGE

The dead
Underneath us;
They get out once in
A blue moon.

—JULES LAFORGUE

She never closes her eyes
So I don't get any sleep
Her daydreams
Eclipse the sun
Make me laugh as well as make me cry
And talk when I don't have a single thing to talk about

—PAUL ÉLUARD

Pale Muse, after me again!
You ask way too much.
It's like writing on sand

In the middle of a storm.
I remember when I was young
And poems just came.
But things have gotten tough;
My instrument would snap like a reed
If I so much as tried.

—ALFRED DE MUSSET

The art of poetry, the mechanical arts, love, the art of being a grandfather and dancing, seeing as an art, the art of accomplishment, the caressed (and caressing) art, Japanese woodcuts, playing at art, edible art, the art of the torturer.

—PAUL ÉLUARD

The doctors always get it wrong:
I can't begin to think straight
Unless I'm drowning in wine.

—PIERRE DE RONSARD

the horses kicked up pieces of a dream
big red clouds mushroomed
over the public spaces
even the small streetlamps swiveled their beacons to see
as for the future its lethal mosquitoes whined and steamed
  in the gardens

—AIMÉ CÉSAIRE

Write on behalf of the smells and the wind
Write on behalf of the leaf's silver
You don't want any donkey-faced human
Doing the looking or understanding or breathing

—PIERRE JEAN JOUVE

Ah these states of being there isn't even a name for, Alps of the soul, mental fogs and infinitesimal misfires which are my daily bread, ah this fact-obsessed race—I repeat myself and don't seem to get very far and still I outdo you, you assholes, perfect pigs, maestros of inexactness and worse, trussers-up of portraits, hack writers, night crawlers, worshippers of unripeness, professors of insects, ah nemeses clinging to every word out of my mouth.

—ANTONIN ARTAUD

Misfortune my old colleague,
Have a seat,
Take a load off,
Relax and I will too.
("I order you: RELAX")
Let's really get to know one another.
You bite the dust.

My opera house, my harbor, my soul.
My cave lined with gold.
Future life, true mother, everything out there.
In your immense light (my horror)
I let go.

—HENRI MICHAUX

The avenue stretches itself out and yawns . . . A train hoots from behind a row of hedges . . .

—LÉON-PAUL FARGUE

They're all at the dinner table
But no one is eating
They don't touch their plates
Which are standing at attention
In back of their heads.

—JACQUES PRÉVERT

Autumn, bed-ridden and loved

—GUILLAUME APOLLINAIRE

It's not nearly as enjoyable to write something down as it is to erase it in one fell swoop like a sudden storm. Cut to black.

—FRANCIS PONGE

U, ups and downs, unfathomable pulse of green seas,
The peace of grazing animals, and of the lines
Alchemy publishes on students' foreheads . . .

—ARTHUR RIMBAUD

To have all the words
Running around in one's head
And choose the plainest if not the worst
And then start the celebration

—JULES SUPERVIELLE

Cinémathèque

I mean, who isn't heating up for the next life
on the order of Antoine Doinel, or a pot of unsweetened
    chocolate.
Beginning with a single window and the sense
that what we know outgrows everything except a headache
or the desk dreaming on its own. It doesn't matter
if being upright brings living beings closer to
the lives they lead (one's 26-year-old self smokes a cigar
but isn't a desperado) nor is beginning a poem with
someone's wrath a means of stepping outside the self
as though volume equalled flesh tones—any more than the Epic of
the Roast Chicken with Lyonnaise potatoes and Buttered Greens
takes over the above-ground, colors and smells pushed aside.

Six Impromptus

Probity? What's the point
of being so down after being so up
What am I a sun?

⋆

Hard to tell if touch—*touch*—
is a part of what is really there
and not just a part of what it feels like
to think so.

⋆

To the medium-sized maple tree, probably Norway
with the old moon in its arms.
Wobbling but adjusting for, chiefly,
things. Pangs too, but not chiefly: no offense

(or hint) to "the person I want to say it"
I want to say discordantly.

⋆

(Please don't talk about me when I'm gone)
Back in a jiff!
If a drink can be a
Bloody Mary, why can't a cloud,
stunted and pocked, be a world view. Because I say so?

The daffodil with the color variation,
arms long and small.

⋆

Thick blue but it isn't air or paint. Or sorrow.
Amsterdam Ave. with its churches sneaking past St. Luke's
    Hospital
on its way to the fortress of Columbia (walled and domed)

which sneaks off to a lecture at Yale.
Architecture between then and there.

⋆

The three favorite winter hours
striding up sunny Broadway

so why isn't my heart
dancing. It's a wonder more people
(and crosstown buses) don't get lost
once they fall in, which is another way
of conceding transitional states, the
alpha and omega of measure

to the jazz alto player
with the classical training.

Replies to Paul

(Limitedness)

Life is clearly a gift like the ballpoint pen from TSL,
Time and Space Ltd. in Hudson, N.Y., info@timeandspace.org
rather than from the *TLS* which ups the subscription rate every
time you renew,
but given that the pen is at least ten years old, the email
could well have changed along with the other info printed on it
like the air I stepped into not five minutes ago, a thick cloud
of absence.
If, as I think, life is more a family of resemblances
than a notion bounded by what it includes and excludes,
it comprises a lot of under/over that exceeds any reasonable
notion of limitedness
relevant to either time or space, so the important events
(some of them pretty clearly embarrassed to be taking part
hence the gusts, distant rumblings, sun showers, etc.)
occur above and below any reasonable notion of ground. So say
the faceless clouds over the woods, one red almost to the point
of violet
another losing traction close to the cable tower barely in
silhouette.

(Winged Purposes)

No one lives in a can of Italian tomatoes with a red and blue
  label
for long; and even if you do it's rare
to wake up swimming in European references.
"Carfax," for example, which I just learned
from reading the beautiful, poignant journals of Denton Welch
(July 27, 1943, the air swarming with "doodlebugs")
means four-way corner, from the Middle English *carfuks*
and ultimately from the Latin *quadrifurcus*, more formal
than substantial, as Denton Welch's impossibly short life
virtually gives the lie to substance. This is partly in memory of
  him.
Also of the spring philosophy week in Oxford (courtesy of Ted)
whose Carfax Tower is a landmark for philosophers
and everyone else. (Possible worlds, pay attention.)
Pasternak would cue the snow and the pigeons. Francis Ponge, John
  Wheelwright,
Larry Fagin, Richard Kolmar, Emily Greenley . . . in a single line,
  please.
No pet projects and no romance of Beaux Arts facades
—though not unpleasant in spite of the cold, smoky gray. Past
the scrawny bones of Christmas trees piled close to the curb
for future soup, beside the brushed-in sun.

(Henry VIII)

You can fit everything I know onto a postcard of Poughkeepsie.
Well, a couple.
The moon buzzing the torn spruce branches
if not taking its place with all the people in hair-curlers
lined up in front of the Catskills.
Scylla mated with Charybdis yesterday
but the trajectory is to leave things in their bedraggled state,
the classically trained percussionist moonlighting as a rosebush
or a stump, and the ordinary landscape making a quick exit like
    the pool table it is.
Speaking of which, the season of the trombone isn't nearly as
    pushed to an extreme
as the hero whose job it is to get up and make the coffee,
and toast if possible, while it little profits
to avoide squabbles in the pit
or bend (like any of Anne Boleyn's attendants) to the whispered
blandishments that leave so little behind that's tangible, even
    if petted.

Piece of a Rhapsody

The dawn turns into a maple tree then a fakebook from the windy 1940s then back into dawn and speaks. It would be nice if writing as well as reading took a lot less time. That by the way is chapter one. With the net out, shaded in or not, and the sadder exclamations, sprocket and well-wisher, sending a pigeon as an envoy. Just in case. As for the suggestion that the natural world is no more constructed than a Plan de Paris, it was followed by a thin cloud of reddish smoke, more plum than scarlet, spattered by daylight.

Elevenses

for collaboration with Trevor Winkfield

APRIL 10. Opening Day

though it's been proved time and time again that few things close
entirely, mouths, screen doors, seasons, hearts, cases, bars, flies
(I know: minds, plays, arteries, bookstores . . .)

JUNE 22. The giraffe vendor stopped by and will come back later. He seems nice. Granting the difference between a wish and a "forward gesture," does a flashback constitute a new element, rather than a celebration of continuity? Is it like taking it from the top in music?

JUNE 26. Speaking of names for new elements, what about Equilibrium at 11:00 a.m.—not exactly a solid but by no means a gas. Can an emulsion be an element? Wittgensteinium? Stradivarium?

JUNE 29. Tedium, Lineoleum, Hegemony, Ilium, Brookynese,
Subfusc, Simulacrum, Granola, Dopamine, Honorarium,
Ephithalamion, Byzantium, Secretariat, Incunabula,
  Praeludium,
Exxon, Saturnalia, Rustoleum, Leafmold, Facture,
Plebiscite, Lager, Monadium, Parsimony, Segovia,
Pogrom, Irony, Cognate, Rabbinate, Horror vacui,
Atonality, Timbre, Pasta, Metope, Uterine,

Valparaiso, Borax, Exemplum, Laputa, Assam,
Aileron, Kleenex, Avarice, Gesso, Mucilage,
Modicum, Opprobrium, Occam, Pesticide, The Blues

Names are over-rated anyway. (A small brownish-blackish bird just galloped away without one.)

JUNE 30. You can lead a paper wasp to a coffee cup

but you can't know if circling the rose-colored rim has anything to do with the creative process, or if a rush of cool air storms a previously unacknowledged barricade (it is, after all, only two weeks to Bastille Day) rattling the edges of everything except—strictly speaking—what doesn't have any.

JULY 7. The chrysalis, the chain, the giraffe, the palette, the melon, the vase, the red bows, the roosters, and the blockhouse (or bunker) are parts of the innermost life like Beethoven's *Grosse Fugue*.

Oh?

AUGUST 4. Use "footling" in a sentence.

Her footling friend phoned twice while she was out looking for the plastic twine.

Catcalls from the spruces, who know we aren't up to their standards even when they're bereft, which so many are.

AUGUST 10. What about the winds of staying the same

or does Fate get too much press as it is, apart from its celebrated multiple personality disorder. Why limit participants to three? Why no distinctions along the lines of the Muse of Restless Desire and the Reckless Past?

AUGUST 11. The late morning of the poem. Meaning—not dawn, noon, dusk, the wee small hours, etc.

AUGUST 25. When you are old and gray and full of medicinal properties

on the Street of Dreams. I think that's a take?

We can expand it later.

SEPTEMBER 8. Yes! about the publisher logo. I've always liked, even envied a little, the self-satisfaction, including the puffing up

whereas the famous penguin always looks a bit out of it, don't you think? Wanting to take the first step but not sure if it will work (pulled over for a sobriety test?). I find myself wanting to push it over like a schmoo—I hope that doesn't sound mean-spirited!

SEPTEMBER 21. The Day of the Low Relief. Wolf gone, island gone, saw-horses gone, corrosives gone—and forgotten. Bunkers dropping like flies.

SEPTEMBER 27. ("Autour de mes cartes . . . ") The Rodchenko Mayakovsky one from so long ago—looking daggers at the world in an uncomfortable-looking suit and tie and dangling a brimmed hat and a cigarette from long fingers. His wooden chair pushed back against a bare wall (thin wainscotting) is clearly too small for someone his height. High-top laced shoes glued to scratched floorboards while he waits, handsome, wary, and aggressive, for the next question about his work, his loves, and his changing relationship to the Party.

SEPTEMBER 30. Disambiguation: An Inkling

not *The Inklings*, who met in a semi-formal, or at least regular, manner at the Bird and Baby (Eagle and Child) pub on St. Giles St. in Oxford in the—1930s?—most notably C.S. Lewis and Tolkien. From *ink* as well as hint? Jimmy would know. The pub figures in Colin Dexter's Inspector Morse mysteries. When we were there it was packed, not easy to place an order (in front, with no room for people to get around you) or navigate the narrow aisle to the other end

of summer. In the air mostly, given cold wet grass and cold earth. Is it ever not? (Does nature never get embarrassed?) Inklings in smells, breezes, sudden clearings, ejaculations. Why did the ox ford the stream here? To get to the other quad.

NOVEMBER 1. Some ideas are nearer and dearer than others, the problem is how to make them permanent and not just "souped up" for the occasion. With the corollary that permanence is, to at least some degree, a function of souping up. Take the one about daylight supported by nothing until you and I realize we're the ones chosen to carry it, along with the grocery bags, paper coffee cups, and list of things that really should be done by lunchtime. Ideas that can't—or won't—adjust to the times gust into oblivion without so much as a blink (the Seven Civic Dwarfs, half the bunk house, Porrex and Ferrex, the Hotel de Dream, the rooster crowing its head off—I'm scratching the surface).

NOVEMBER 15. A smell of garlic

and the almost sun leans on a linden tree, affecting nonchalance.

NOVEMBER 19. The silent *e* that looks back at you from the ends of so many words, though I have a suspicion it doesn't always do so happily.

NOVEMBER 20. Pale green celery leaves and the smaller, whitish hearts that signify narcissism in the unmediated sense—but I only recently learned that *narcotic* has the same root, which might explain to some degree those mornings when fog, for want of a better term, is unrelieved. What is the 'good life' apart from focus on what is good about it for as long as that lasts, absent which the notion has so little content or connection to the conscious self that the smallest breeze or grinding of brakes puts an end to it? Of course, horse radishes and turnips are hearts too (never mind artichokes); possibly Macoun apples with their short season; whereas the outer-directed eggplants, carrots, kale, tomatoes, pumpkins, etc., live healthy and useful lives reveling in "Monopoly" colors. As do cars and national flags.

NOVEMBER 22. A living sea of waking dreams doesn't sound *so* bad, does it? Wouldn't it depend on the nature of the dreams? We're asleep most of the time anyway, as someone said—probably not Bishop Berkeley. Walnut with a hint of maple.

NOVEMBER 27. Charms #3 and #4 but it might re-set. A dose of lunch! The machine obliterates half the words before their lips.

DECEMBER 2. It isn't sadness at least I don't think so. The think tank was named, but tendentiousness is crescent-shaped, self-conscious about its role in mental activity, so propping it up is smearing nothing on top of nothing. 1. Out the door and forgotten. 2. The glyph. 3. Faces gone purple. 4. Manchester and Leeds.

DECEMBER 11. The Morning of the Villanelle (or: "The Death of Albertine"). The individual is lost in the mass, neither more nor less visible. Desire colors from first to last. Evidence of a clouded past whose points of view were barely tenable, the individual is lost in the mass the way the present is its own forecast: February pushed into April whose desire colors from first to last. When in the course of humans en masse each is, theoretically, isolable, the individual is lost in the mass. Nothing is too vast including the wish to be exceptional (desire colors from first to last) burning off morning mist (art at its most unstable) while the individual is lost in the mass, colored by desire from first to last.

DECEMBER 12. Antlers in the treetops . . . nope just a rooster with prongs. Does one 11 o'clock shade into the next? It's not private—

exactly—but neither is it open for viewing like some coffins or an eye in the pocket of a catcher's mitt. Grayish blue and intent.

DECEMBER 13. Sounds of early love-making on the backlot.—*Cut that.* I will. Later.

DECEMBER 14. The day, after being scooped out of its trough, mostly by hand but with some heavy machinery too, was rolled out, tarred, cemented, and allowed to dry before traffic resumed its normal morning flow on both sides of Broadway and the other north-south arteries that define the West Side. While it's true that names make navigating easier, it's also true that most are merely pasted on—occasionally romantically involved with their subjects, but more often creatures of habit or even sheer impulse.

As the Nominalist said to the morning rubbing its eyes in Monument Valley before heading due East: Reach for the skies!

(Jump cut to Chopin and George Sand in front of a big picture window on Mallorca.)

DECEMBER 16. Conjugate "futz" (as in "futz around").

If time is essentially shorthand for the future, have a look at the pencil-thin buildings on the drawing board, hard to erase is my guess, let alone providing a window to a caress.

DECEMBER 17. (Note from yesterday.) The rusted water tank with the cupola and its imagined pendentives at 4:00 p.m.

vs. the screen saver—when encroaching darkness is the last thing you want saved. One of the things a Bloody Mary clearly has going for it is the color. More too of course, but the free-floating passion (when used, shaved ice a reminder of the "frozen sea" within) in contrast to the physicalist celery or explosiveness of Tabasco (red darkened upon red) touches more deeply than mere alcohol.

Sez you.

Well, I do. I think. Who knows. Not the moon swirling in the clouds of its gray matter, or the migrainous sun suffused with an Analytical Cubism of meanings, in color and not, like a fireball hitting a window pane. Part of what I think is that texture, grain, *feel* are days of the week, and the formal aspects that used to count as bare-bones reality scoop years from the lives they're glued to. There goes one now. Nothingness, the Sinfonietta they all play in, pauses just long enough for spacetime to get a word in

before the sun dips a toe into the glass and the blood sprouts wings, claws and a beak, and pushes off from its high-rise perch for parts unknown to the perceiver who perceives the redness that is not, before being blindsided by the redness that is.

Aria for Michael Gizzi

How long the thin terrain resolutely
ground—well, you could leave the world
precisely as it's reflected, the fringes
poking through empires of June and
allover lateness, a condition the issuers
fought over while swimming in open air.
It has its paint smell and its newsletter.
The embers getting out from underneath the charm
are the French door to others, ivy on tenterhooks,
onion grass fobbed off onto mid-morning.
Produce your siren! Also the telephone
book to take to the hotel with the aisle
of lilac light looking like a mountain lake.
Or a strait. Why not sheer deadline
closer than red lips to Venetian glass.

After Pasternak

Stop it this instant!
Or what.
The cartoon heavies collecting in the mall.
The endless ride to St. John's and the reddening beyond

which doesn't throw light
on why, with so much involved,
the earth doesn't leave *us*.
Peel off, like the beautiful cold weather of the past few days.

Take the roofs open to everything
including snow and rain.
Even the lintels get weary
for all their shoulderings and narrow

if steadfast view of what's to come, edged
with gingko trees and a few nameless shrubs.
A shaft of sunlight cutting through!
The city climbs in backwards through the kitchen window.

Desk

for Kenneth Koch

Desk: I am the whole desk, the couch for everything.

Desk From Above: I am the varnished top. Don't write about me!

Varnish: The daylight's wish (realism's splash).

Disk: O Saussure!

Olivetti Lettera 32: I am not Italian I am from Spain but I
remain the writer's writer's writer.

Jaw-Shaped Stapler: I remind myself of the old U. of Alabama and
later NFL QB Ken ("The Snake") Stabler.

Post-It: The poster boy of the past.

Box Of Post-Its: Cherry, lime, eggplant, squash, banana,
tangerine, and every other food color known to humans.

Gooseneck Lamp With Clamp: What are you trying to hide?

Paperclip: I join things at the hip.

One-Inch Paper Clamp: Democracy has to turn its eye on itself periodically if it is to function politically, socially, economically, ethically, even (many would say) logically.

Coffee Mug: I am the coffee's mug, the brain's *kisser.*

Saucer: Although virtually invisible in the normal course of things, I never think of myself as infra dig.

Drawer In Quotes: I am the one and only drawer-like space underneath the hinged piano lid of a top: the score for inner voices: the artist along with the model, brushes, tubes of paint, and various mediums: O mousse of possible worlds!

Metal Mesh Wastebasket: As everyone knows, the task is to get around me.

Digital Alarm Clock: I don't hate you! I try to remain neutral.

Words From KK: In a 3" x 5" spiral notebook with a green cover (1967).

The Poem I Meant To Write: Love me or leave me and let me be lonely!

Postcards Taped To The Wall Behind: Vladimir Mayakovsky, Pee-wee Herman, *The Avenue at Middelharnis,* the cover of *La Doublure* by Raymond Roussel, excerpt from Dorothy Wordsworth's

Journals, *Still Life with Fruit and Vegetables* by Cotán, *Chambre de Stéphane Mallarmé*, *Superbia* by Brueghel, etc.

The Perfect Poem: I am the perfect poem inside the desk, though not in the shallow drawer-like space underneath the top, not taped to the wood or the metal hinge, and not accessible while the desk exists in its present form.

Typewriter Ribbon: I am the inky tabula rasa, the Red Carpet for the poem to come.

Blue Plastic Box With Stamps, Ink Pad, Return Address Stamp, Pilot Pen, And Pocket Calculator: The desk's corner mailbox.

File Cabinet: If wishes were horses, false starts would be Secretariat!

Photo Of Jimmy Schuyler (In His Twenties?): I am the desk's inspiration's heart's springtime. The (poet's poet's) Eiffel Tower's vista's meadow strewn with early crocuses and dandelions.

Scotch Tape And Scissors: Highly rated surgical team.

Portable Fan: (1) Being's respiration. (2) The wind in closeup.

Words From KK #2: John Ashbery prefers to "sneak out" of a poem.

William Carlos Williams: What girl will care / for us, do you
think, if we continue in these ways?

Wallace Stevens: I'm stuck inside the binding!

Ballpoint Pen: The *functional* point of the past.

Green Magic Marker: Hooo!

Felt-Tip: Whatever happens, regardless, happens for a reason.

NYU Retractable Ballpoint Pen (Gift From Mike): Washington Square
Park framed in the moment's leafy *plein air.*

Keats Paperweight: I am the one with the well known Severn
portrait. I wish I could but I can't prevent ideas for poems—
or anything else—from blowing away.

Ex-Watchdog Takes Powder

The days go by without you. But they know you know.
Like the effulgent gods who might be interested in us
if they gave it half a chance.

Just when you start thinking
that how something seems is as important
as what it is responsible to believe about it

Mayakovsky enters in a shirt the color of winter sunlight.

The traditional categories, wanderlust, organ food,
    nothingness,
enlist the new century in their crusade.
Fleeting as covered wooden bridges, which are also crusade-like.

Names In November

for John Koethe

1.

Sturdy but pale, like an upcoming memorial.
Fifth Avenue gets dragged downtown and the nominalists
enjoy the ride the same way the actual names do. No profile
in peril, only occasionally the confusing view above
the Harlem and East Rivers, lurching but undeniably smitten.

The barest hint of green moves a taxi
with a sliding door to the curb, from which
the great pianist Alfred Cortot steps into the crosswalk,
head bent so nothing is on film, or awkward with strangers.

2.

Christopher Wren, Butterfly McQueen, Robin Roberts,
Angel Cordero—where are you when we need you!
The dream sends out for a street. Not enough.
At least names give it a shape.

The poetry is too much with us.—You can't say that.
Knobby certainty, reticent about its affect
which includes endless sputtering from the bridge traffic below.
Take the noble gases, the cream-colored Mercedes barely grazed by
evening.
Prey to rugged individualism like the Hermes typewriters.

Variations

1.

O.k. you can't say it just as you can't say
time passes or passed yesterday or is around the corner,
almost here. The day is scratchy not impossible. It did
some skipping in the morning but calmed down by lunch.
What is the smallest unit that can be considered lyrical
but not sentimental. Grassy as a backyard,
separated like people despite their relentless
shading into one another, appealing as objects that
can stand on their own without undue wobbling or confusion

2.

Nor as long as we're on the subject is it
exactly true to say that poems or lives are abandoned
rather than finished however that jibes with current procedure.
Sometimes what appears to be abandoned was finished
and then taken up again, etc., reinstatement
producing not quite identity but groupings having to do
with qualities as vague as aura or "feel"
—a better way of saying that might be that differences
in style—bumps in the road—are part and parcel of overall flow
and as such fit the predisposition to patterning that
enables general qualities, including solace, to become
essentials in the ongoing search for tangible resolution

3.

The related question of how long meanings
actually last is at least as muted as where an
answer would leave us—not, hopefully, all but buried
beneath expectations that ride roughshod over what was clear
at the outset: that of the myriad ways to talk about
what can't finally be resolved, some have their basis in feeling
others permit understanding to be only as coherent
as those who indulge in it, and a good portion
of the rest occupy a position on the fault line between
tone and logic quite apart from whatever vogue (tinged as it
may be by habits of long standing) for sequence as in
the scratchiness which I referred to earlier, regardless
of what seems and for all practical purposes is the case

4.

To transpose to things—how long they persist
and whether or not what we understand as persistence
is smooth or rough or some unlikely coalition of the two
permeating the wish for solace, whether on the thin side
like winter shade or displayed in piercing daylight; and
whether the gradual underlining of the idea that
we are contributors to this view as much as recipients
stacks the deck

5.

Objections aside, the so-called verbs of being
continually approach a precipice which has
less to do with depth or immediacy than faraway
implications soaked with skin, teeth, eyesight, etc.
A basis in other words, but one whose deference to the present
masks endless gaps in much the same way appearance,
despite its well known devotion to us and all
we accomplish, has one foot in forecasts that can't possibly be
    accurate
at least to the degree most of us hope and pray for

6.

The long road which forgetfulness may
wander, which doesn't stop anyone from persisting
but does produce a ground bass of expectancy that
brandishes even while it pretends to pull back, with the most
 obvious
consequences. Not that goals are continually being
redistributed within an identifiable range
but that the resulting physics plows into the time line
with such force that the axes are too much with us,
separating progress from habit, high-rises from the rolling
 playing field
that takes in economic and social forces as much as untitled need

7.

Anyone can write an ode to behavior on the part
of creatures whose originals, by and large, keep to themselves.
Muster the caring, each judgment strained to the
point of obloquy—before snagging on the recentness
of the past in question, together with its programmers
and strayed verbs ganging up on what used to seem
sewn in such a way that the on-again off-again
relation to privacy that forms a purchase on so much
still to be framed is skimmed off like the merest dawn,
i.e., abandoned prior to being cut down to make room
for all that glistens in front, loss as much sequence,
while the credits stream overhead

Ashcan

for John Godfrey

As the acanthus tree said to the vacant lot
(difficult to translate—)

draws heavily. It isn't Ravel.
The sidewalk with the meadow

This is the talent just ears
and the past pushing off (pushed in turn)

They have this talking awning
out of time's cant

sans feet, sans name
sans embouchure, sans everything

short of a view
from the Bayonne Bridge.

So it's late.
Souls strewn at mealtimes

And as for poems terminable and interminable
hand out the piece

That's just it, it
isn't a world of givenness

papery, veined, Gozzano
to the beautiful Georgian-style

what it's *like*
to be a duck's back

The line separating
squirrels and impromptu

but it jumps—pink
as a speaking part

the nape pre-everything
for each brass mute

waffling on Ashcan
you can almost touch it

Trio

1. Lee Wiley Sings Schubert

As belle of the rooftops
—partly, I'm sure, because
ambient longing is the world view.
One of the views.
It's eerie to see it watched over
like a construction site.
The robins raise their glasses—late for sweeping
change but each shiver
rolls the tape.
(*Tucket within.*)

2. Allegro Tristamente

How do you know time *isn't*
the tacet and space
the realistic mode of determining
what will and won't fulfill the requirements?

What would you say to
less fuss about the moon
and consequent toppling (you with the landscape
carved up into swamp maples and hailstorms of pinks).

3. Seeing Is

You say tomato
and I say the world is troubled
profoundly and we
see only what protrudes

through a lens clouded
with all nobody wants to see
so the cloud is phenomenologically
prior and the trouble takes over this much
and then more and if global
warming re-supplies it head-on
the loss of life surging from underneath
is believing, it doesn't matter when
it climbs on.

Study for "Everything"

Tenure schmenure the sages are all on the Hudson River pier.
  Don't lean over too far.
I wouldn't be surprised to see arms and legs, even a vital organ
  or two
representing the shy—passive-aggressive—inner life.
Brushing out followed by. . . brushing in.

If people in high-rises shouldn't groan
neither should the brownstones huddle closer together
each time there's a hint of autumn in the air or in the trees—
like, if you'll pardon me for saying so,
rushing to cremate the dead when everyone,
themselves included, knows we want them around for as long as
  humanly possible.

Not, of course, that the pangs have much choice
regarding where to settle, or be observed.
A rusty hydrant is as good as a park bench.
The handful of pigeons poking around a chunk of baguette near
  the grass
don't seem to agree, but they're hand-stamped,
inks (some line, too?) already beginning to fade.

I only know what I know is one version.
Another—as witness so many royal portraits

or the parade of experimental drugs
for a dread disease—is that knowledge works only some of the
time.
Really works. Never mind how things
seem as opposed to how they see themselves, or why
appearance stakes so much if not everything on the distinction.

Everything

> "Everything is just nothing repeating
> itself."
>
> —GEORGE HERRIMAN

1

Stop me if you've heard this one.
Two llamas poke their heads out of the small stone enclosure
(part of a garage) they spend their time in
when they're not taking the sun in a
tiny, fenced-in yard dotted with wildflowers.
Just as we turned to look, a small flock
of wild turkeys materialized out of nothing
and began squawking, clearly at us.
Who knew they were the concierge family!

Everything gusts—
and then dies back down.

At least as likely: Everything exists
inside a giant thought balloon
which rides continual gusts, although no one
can possibly speak about, let alone contemplate, the
situation.
As to the air outside the balloon, spangled
with oak leaves and high strips of white clouds . . .

let's leave that one for now.

As the beaver said to the log half in, half out of water,
getting to gnaw you. Getting to gnaw all about you.

Speaking of balloons, the image I've always liked,
from as far back as high school, is the lead one.
Successful as a lead balloon.
It took off: like a lead balloon.
The fact that it got off the ground at all
—before plummeting with a thud if not a loud crash—
does a good job of encapsulating human striving
wedded to human failure. Not, certainly, that the conjunction
is inevitably the case. But the poignancy,
to me anyway, is palpable.

As to the light from outside that must penetrate the thought
    balloon
regardless of its color or degree of translucence,
that, too, seems best left for later,
like playing two sets of tennis following a bout of pneumonia.

Or the view of Niagara that nobody has.

What did the 20-oz. bottle of Perrier
say to the late afternoon sunlight struggling to get indoors?
The apartment building has more openings than the sprawling
cemetery on the way to the dump upstate

or the one littering the heavily-trafficked Manhattan
approach to the Robert F. Kennedy (formerly Triboro) Bridge.
You'd think the fumes by themselves would be a discourager!

You say tomato
and I say everything is consumed by its appearances.
I've been instructed to push
a handful of minor characters back into the wings but they won't
go,
no matter how hard I try.
The pencil line between being and not being, hardly
static however it looks

—more accurately, between staying put
and erupting into feelings that can't be held in check no matter
what,
like the corruption built into medical advertising
aimed directly at the TV-viewing public—

reminds me of the boundary line
between so-called feeling and so-called understanding.
To have a purchase on. Know thoroughly
by close contact with, or long experience of,
as opposed to hearsay or even legitimate authority.
As the great poet Mayakovsky sidestepped at least some
of the more sinister aspects of Futurism, only to fall victim to
himself

as well as comrades who didn't mean nearly as well as
they should have, so time fights off just about every
conjunction,
those with palpable connections to space
as well as just about any others you can name.

There goes one now.

"No. It's a bird batting by."

In fact the sky,
as Wallace Stevens remarked of the world
just prior to the onset of World War II (in contrast to
T. S. Eliot whom Stevens somewhat surprisingly singles out for
praise)
is growing floppier. Warped tent poles and stakes,
an occasional scrawny pigeon on the wing,
one roof garden with a flapping umbrella
which, from the back, looks like Our Lady of the George
Washington Bridge

but no cloud structure for support, unless you count the grayish
wisps,
barely clouds, that hung around the Palisades
for most of the morning. Actually, the view is appealing—
provided it doesn't decide to go
too far in the direction of floppiness
and risk falling over into the appearance

of whatever is holding it up, a girder or pylon
or some idea of structure per se that hasn't yet been
"instantiated."

Speaking of support, I've had a hard
time forgetting about the guy in our building
who I used to see going for his run every morning before
breakfast,
who jumped from his tenth-floor window and magically survived,
seriously broken bones but alive, apparently
because he landed in a tiny courtyard on a bale
of recycled newspapers, primarily *The New York Times.*

Does that qualify as the ethical sphere? Maybe just?

Yesterday morning just before I woke up,
a few persons with backpacks and what looked like metal maps
several inches thick
were bobbing up and down on platforms that looked like ice floes
but more cork than ice. Every once in a while
one of them went over with a silent splash.

Suicide is one of the silent *e* words
but so are cope and rosette.
Inchoate. Baseline. Nape.

Here's one. How many singularities
can fit onto the head of a pin

pushed into the so-called bulletin board of consciousness
(cork again but not a real theme, I'm pretty sure)

as distinct from the riptides, sinkholes, tsunamis, you name it
(occasionally just a tone row or cluster)
that emerge, seemingly out of nothing,
to manhandle the attention principle and hold on
for what can seem, and in some cases be, hours or even entire
    days?

So how best to use one's time
—which in one very large sense is everything—
is at best a conundrum worth examining
and at worst the exam in the dream (with all the silent
    percussion)
in the course you've never signed up for, although
everyone else is scribbling away at their desks next to their
green lamps: the *lagniappe* being (somewhat on the order of dusk)
an apparently new range of colors, intonations, shapes, etc.,
which is familiar and also entirely out of the blue.

2

As I was saying

The art of schmoozing isn't hard to master.
— I wasn't saying that you were!
Well, stop anyway.

Two beefsteak tomatoes go out for a walk
just before sunset, avoiding anything with sharp edges: shadows
of pre-war cornices and iron gates
on the relatively bright pavement,
grates, high heels, stop signs,
the shark kite stuck between tree branches . . .

Blood-red thoughts . . .

which don't include, although they hint at,
certain of the silent *e* words
I began to mention earlier—suffused if
not with blood, then with a coursing nostalgia for beginnings.
Sometimes unbearably so.

Orange, absence, muse, landscape, still-life.
Ductile, imbibe, force, nerve, musculature.

Compared to which *clichés*
teem with life,

like the blood-red peppers that stretch a Meléndez landscape
cum still-life to the bursting point.

Just because a
single letter appears with more frequency
than any other letter in the alphabet, it doesn't mean its
    position
is always the most enviable—

any more than black A, white E, red I,
green U, and blue O
are written in stone, Rimbaud notwithstanding.
In fact, in the version I prefer,
every one of those backwards-looking, forlorn-seeming final *e*'s
was wrenched from its quarry of pink granite

as from the age of eight
(and probably before)
the urn-like U has been firmly cemented
in the yellow-orange range, if not so dark
or coarse-grained—*painterly* is the word—
as the orangey hawk that used to land on our bedroom air-
    conditioner
three or four times a year, whether to
gather its energy or look down onto the street
for a meal, or just decide on the next leg of the trip.

What is it like to be a hawk?

What would it be like to see things
too clearly, from above as well as below?

I hope the following isn't depressing,
but the more I entertain it
the more I like the image of a coffin with a skylight,
as the writer Michel Leiris described the lid
Raymond Roussel had made for his mother, presumably
so he could have glimpses of her
even after the coffin was nailed shut for good.

Death thou shalt die.

Or at the very least
be an open and not eternally closed case.
A lot more poignant
—and human, it seems to me—
than desperate. What it is
like to be something rather than nothing.

George Herriman: "Everything is just nothing repeating itself."

I know that's Krazy Kat
(actually, it's the inspiration of Bum "Bill" Bee,
a dour but oddly engaging resident
of Herriman's Coconino County, Arizona),
but the point, I hope, is that

the substitution of daylight for dark,
everyday experience for the mystery that threatens
to bury it out of time and out of mind
("the nothing that is")
is worth acres of literary allusions.

Speaking of mysteries—
the literary kind and not merely the "ultimate" one—
it occurred to me that trying
to write one is a way of separating
what is important from what certainly isn't;
what the Detective Chief Inspector had for breakfast
along with his espresso (in Paris,
where most of the action takes place),
the color of his forties-style trenchcoat and the sky
louring over the centuries-old buildings

alongside the deadly game being played out over fictional time
which is organized into chapters that are both
artificial and also gripping segments of real life
—and whose very artificiality the reader
perceives as a way of providing not only
a convenient framework for the reading experience,
but hints (on some level) about facing
actual situations that might prove overwhelming,
e.g., the notion that a penultimate chapter may embrace
the future as well as the present, thereby
mediating any untenable shocks to the system.

A few additional examples along the same lines
(we might call it "domesticating"
what is profoundly other): the notion of an underworld,
quaint as that is; people dropping
"like flies"; a headless figure in a black cloak
carrying a tool used for harvesting;
the image of a coffin open to sunlight, if not fresh air.

I don't mean to suggest
that profound mysteries have no elements lingering
in the air or on the grass like dew
—or bullet casings—

not to speak of shreds of last night's dream
which, unsurprisingly, was mostly about you. My position was
unclear.

"The trouble with mornings is that they come when you're not
awake."—Archie Goodwin

But rarely if ever
is it everything or nothing—just as
it's never Archie Goodwin without Nero Wolfe, and rarely
without the wonderful, mysterious Saul Panzer as well.

Or Scylla without Charybdis.
Or anagnorisis or *fate* accompli, but not both.

I hasten to add that if you have anything to say about any of
this
which might be of interest to others
and not just yourself (or your in-group)
by all means say it. But please remember
to raise a hand and wait to be recognized. Others may be
as eager to speak—or object—as you are,
and the time, as always, is limited.

3

November 16. Breezy, blue, radiant
but not that radiant.
The Day of the Projectionists

toppling onto the hard wooden seats below.

Let's go back to the time that passes
leaving clumps of time in its wake,
and up ahead still more time—clumps and even Grand Concourses
    of it.

It's still early. Hard to tell if the morning
which thrashed around for several hours
before settling down, not exactly
for a nap, is holding a grudge
and if so on behalf of what. Or whom.

A small apartment building with a crowded
Starbucks at street level,
two Korean grocers sporting green awnings,
shadows flying in pieces out of a tinted bank window like ticker
    tape

vs. the valiant, battered cedars
—some missing an arm or even part of a torso—
the reckless sunset high over the road to the Catskills

and their interesting position between landscape
and painting from life (real life vs. "subsistence")

not to mention the so-called
Super Moon which till the past decade
I don't think I was even aware of, let alone its
appearance twice in the same calendar year
and what that might have meant to the Roman poet Lucretius
who believed the moon, like other celestial bodies,
was the same size it appeared to the naked eye.

It's only a Super Moon
underneath a gray flannel sky

but no one wants to spend too much precious time looking up
when so much of importance is firmly below,
the breeze that moves us,
alarming warmth in November and now into mid-December

all of which has been forming a ground,
figuratively as well as (close to) literally.
Something like the ground or *obstinate* bass in much Baroque
    music.

"While darkness, like an ape's face, fell away"
may well be one too many literary quotation (though it is by Hart
    Crane)

but it also suggests that what is below
"carves" reality in a more basic
sense than many are willing to acknowledge.

Of course, I don't mean that there aren't "floaters" of all types
steadily going by, names as well
as what they stand for. Bonded, though the bondings
are frequently applied from without like a crazy glue

in the middle of which Cassiopeia on her wondrous chair
stares past stragglers and would-be petitioners
at her daughter Andromeda who
is staring longingly at Perseus

not that it was ever "silhouettes
silhouettes silhouettes silhouettes
silhouettes silhouettes silhouettes
silhouettes"—and nothing but. Not even in the unpainterly
fifties,
when for all practical purposes everything
was just beginning if not perpetually re-emerging
(everything is just nothing repeating itself)
like Juliet's image of god as fabric shears: take him and cut him
out
in little stars, which certainly sounds like it would hurt.

At least Juliet's radiant aria
calls attention to the sharp contrasts

between thought and action, the eternally divided self
and the difficult carrying out. Not merely
what is projected visually and audibly
but the rosins, frets, corks, ligatures, and valves;
attacks, slurs, glissandos, trills,
fades, cuts, wipes, etc., which accompany
the wildest swings from elation to near-despair
and frequently, if not inevitably, back.

Speaking not just of movies per se
(and assuming you're in earshot
or at least have email access—and will, I know,
keep all of this to yourself),
in my reply the last time
I neglected to mention the film at the modern art museum
about one of my poetic heroes (I know she's
not one of yours and I think I know why
but you should appreciate this anyway)
and why it was disappointing in so many of the ways
documentaries about poets, artists, composers, etc., invariably
are.
For all the good intentions.

One thing I certainly don't want to forget
this time was my surprise at her being
dissed, towards the end of her difficult enough life,

by her great pal and fellow poet! Did you know about that?
We all know he had his problems quite apart from the poetical
ones,
but for some reason I had never heard
about that part of the relationship, had you?

Did you know that she not only drank, but sometimes to unconsciousness?

Talk about the divided soul.
Not that we ever know where the divisions lie
exactly, or what they finally mean
with respect to a life we do know at least something about.

I hope you'll forgive me if I can't
help adding that my map has the Charles River
(and everything to the North of that) but also Division St.,
Granite Corners, The Fellsway, etc.
(Notice I didn't say Mudville.)

Qu'est-ce que vous voulez!

Having a head

and *using* it.—Which means,
among many other things,
fending off what threatens to bury whatever seems promising

if not smash it with
the flat side of a cleaver
like a clove of garlic. Or a whole head.

But to get back to the immediate surroundings,
which are chilly and on the reddish-gray side
with every indication of getting
chillier before we're through . . . it is, after all,
just around the corner from Thanksgiving
which, despite its press, is rarely an easy day to thank.

Of course the thought balloon,
assuming it exists as more than a cartoon
image (or figure of speech)
has something essential to do with all of this,
as it does with time and its repeated rejoinders

which, I can't help reiterating,
have themselves little if anything to do
with maple trees getting ready for winter,
not to mention the van stalled on the ON ramp of understanding.

Or with the assembled sirens
(there are a lot more than generally accounted for)
most of whom would just as soon be home in bed, sleep in as they
    say,
as sing doo-wop to one and all.

Or—nothing, or almost nothing to do with—
the papery covering, thinner than onionskin, over the underworld
which can't be seen or heard or felt,
although its presence is a part of everyone's ordinary experience
in a vital sense, thought balloon or no.

As to the van and related utilities,
if most of us are occupied much less with wrangling gods below or
    above
than with choosing a practical
goal and finding some promising means to achieve it

no one thinks picking out a classic red Corvette with a
    Continental Kit
from the cluster far ahead where the highway begins to curve,
will cure a traffic jam.

To put the big suitcases with the straps,
duffels, carry-ons, backpacks with room for a laptop,
skis and poles, winter jackets, carrier for the cat,
shopping bags from the duty-free shop
and the newspaper/magazine/chotchke stand
onto the trolley, which hopefully won't have anything more piled
    on top
before it reaches its destination

or all your cards on the table.

4

I know what you're thinking—
the *sheerness* of the way everything looks.
A lot more space than necessary

or a lot less filling it, which amounts to the same thing.
For parts of speech as well as people.

Both J. M. W. Turner and Brueghel might have liked it here,
but Babe Ruth actually lived in not one but two of the upscale
 apartment buildings
close to the massive (and hardly noticed these days is my guess)
Soldiers and Sailors Monument, with its view
over the farmland and fairways of northwestern New Jersey
and into eastern Pennsylvania. One of the buildings has his name
 on a plaque outside.

I do know the Babe died relatively young. Do I know what he did
 after baseball?
I could google him . . . maybe later . . .

Sun like a Nerf cheeseburger (can I say that?)

yet a closer look shows too
the orange and reddish-brown sides of corruption.
Tree trunks as well as phone and power lines—

This blond republic . . .

I know it isn't!
But it's windblown, bicameral,
with occasional notes of ice and steel glare

My heart aches and a drowsy numbness
pains my sense, as though of hemlock I had drunk,
or emptied some dull opiate to the drains
one minute past, and Lethe-wards had sunk

Mine too; but I wouldn't
put too fine a point on it,
especially as it's now in the past
along with the overlay, more peeling darkness than emerging sun,
which some time ago resolved itself into a shingled roof
on a small commercial building, most likely a clothes or souvenir
store,
at one corner of what looks like a village square or small
shopping mall

in the middle of which the poetry of alarm,
which I think is what has been making
itself felt, has sat down on a metal bench to catch its breath.

When the moon hits your eye like . . . a Super Moon.
Or a big blob of freshly wrapped mozzarella, dripping with
moisture.

Clearly, no one need be Endymion who doesn't want to be!
Or love the trompe l'oeil
of the life in art à la Keats

who was apparently, according to a biography I recently read,
as ambitious as he was talented.
Well, good for him. No one gets clubbed.

CORPORATE MOGUL CHANNELS BRUEGHEL

But who really, when the chips are down,
would trade space for time, every appearance to the contrary?

If pastiche is, at its root,
an itch for the past . . .

If the old divisions under pressure
to form new and hopefully more practicable ones
align themselves as much with what is
felt as what enters via "repurposing," that horrible
word that is supposed to connote progress
but rarely if ever does (just about anything has the potential
to be not only repeated but worshipped, given sufficient time)

as a half-built apartment building is better,
certainly some would say,
than no prospect at all. Not everything
comes with its appropriate hoopla or

admonitions to be patient . . . just a little while longer . . .
there. Easy does it now.

OK. So where does that leave anyone

apart from, and of course including
everything pasted on top of nothing
as hard as that is to visualize, never mind increased focus
on posterity per se, with end-runs around
categories of steadfastness
and change all the while the taxpayer
beholden to his taxes has a clear enough ground view

but we were talking, at least on and off,
about the sky, which so often seems sure of itself and its
    position
but on closer inspection has other selves
crowding in and demanding to be accounted for—
in fact, doing some shoving right now . . . the Scolded Face,
B-flat, E-flat and C Trumpets, the Palely Brittle Beyond.

As the oral surgeon said after pulling
the wisdom tooth (no pain but audible cracking sensation)

—What's *next*?

Speaking of sensations
you might find this interesting.

A week ago or so ago, there was a layer
of invisible ice coating the side streets which don't
get nearly as much sun as Broadway with an overlay of dry snow
which made walking as treacherous as I can remember.
I almost went down—twice. It couldn't
have been more than a sixteenth of an inch thick,
an underworld like a sheet of artist's acetate

all the while, above,
from sidewalk to firm blue sky,
it was a perfect winter day for New York—everything
in view, nothing wanting or unrepeatable,
no outliers in any meaningful sense.*
If bewitched, then likely to stay that way at least through
    nightfall.

What did the Luminist say to the dream state?
Everything is in Monopoly colors if you'll only look!

Not that some things aren't
sharper, even at a distance, than other things.
I don't mean souped up like space/time
with adjustments not only for gusts
but doldrums too, like the one everybody knows
from Coleridge's "Rime of the Ancient Mariner"; all the mis-
    directions and poor imitations,
factions of hangdog hotel and sheepish grocery awning,

depressing week with art store shuttered because no one buys
    frames (or books).

When illness extrudes "with its careful teeth"
(as the feverish Samuel Greenberg brilliantly put it)
it doesn't mean that life itself is batting .200 or even .225
regardless of the unnatural temperatures
outdoors or the inevitable pressure
to get on with it, bypass the "I did, I think, nothing"
without, in the process, doing an end-run
around what really matters. Name another life.

But it can take practice.

And if, as I keep thinking—

But I keep coming back to the film
over the underworld, thin as a picture plane,
looming (panicky, or producing panic)
as an overhead.

What do the following have in common: The Wright Brothers,
screwball comedies from the late 1930s, the near conjunction of
    mind and body
when the moon hits your eye

like May, or early June.

The excellent new print of Orson Welles's 1940s black-and-white
Chimes at Midnight
collating *Henry IV*, Parts 1 and 2, with *Henry V*
made it even better than expected, even given the sensational cast;
not just John Gielgud and Margaret Rutherford
(cameo by a young Jeanne Moreau of all people)
but the hardly known, to me not at all, Keith Baxter as a thrilling Prince Hal.
It connives at the social fabric without valorizing it.

---

* What has all the earmarks of a crime scene and smells like honeysuckle?
A. Everything.

Coda

Even city planning.

Yesterday, for example,
with its unexpected view of posterity
draped loosely between high-rises
—unlike the composed street
raised to stoop level like a stroller. No moon
but clearly under some pressure to form one in quick stages,
while being careful to avoid what intervenes
with commas, speech tags, etc. Architraves pre-everything.

So that time, or what's left of it,
prior to displaying its secret life (which wasn't so secret to
begin with)
waves everyone and everything away, including the burnished
sills and their plants lithographed with evening

plus the host of secondary qualities that rush in
on the least pretext, a new unit of space,
some jazz below, mouths to feed . . . wrinkles alchemy
prints on studious foreheads. Or indeterminacy.
What did Rimbaud know about ageing anyway?

—More than you think.

Leaving (you might say) a colorful flag without a flagpole,
the parade route all but painted over like the history of un-
    opposed takeovers

and the real wrinkle is that nothing is there for the taking
no matter how it appears. Shuffling off
to Buffalo or wherever they go to fill the intemperate
    intermediate needs,
while the wisps of grass that inevitably push up between cracks
    look digital
and the busses squeeze their passengers to left and right
like shifts in basic economic priorities.

Have I mentioned noodling, as opposed to "raptures of
    "attention"?
The effect without a cause—unless you're one of those
who find that notion empty of meaning—
not only in connection to instrumental music
("I wasn't playing anything I was just noodling")
but phenomena in general, potential as well as kinetic,
from Y. Zowl singing "to a small guitar"
to our near-absorption in textures, weathers, (invasive)
    ellipses, sublimation, etc.?

To sum up: It's not that the telegram to Elizabeth Bishop was
    undelivered
but that the dead—if not busy licking their wounds—

are absorbed with themselves, as we must appear to the
perceptive hawks.
Dark gray, dark green, beet red all over, but also
(hence the notion of collateral damage when it applies)
thickness *tout court.*

Acknowledgments

Portions of "Everything" have appeared in *Bomb, The Brooklyn Rail, Dia Readings in Contemporary Poetry, Hanging Loose*, and *Poetry* (Chicago).

Other poems, in whole or in part, were published in *Court Green, Decals of Desire, Hanging Loose, Poetry* (Chicago), *Sal Mimeo, SpoKe, The Brooklyn Rail,* and *The Delineator.*

Elevenses with art by Trevor Winkfield was published as a limited edition collaboration by Granary Books (New York: 2017).

French Licks was published as a chapbook by Smoke Specs (Seattle: 2019), all translations by the author.

"Ex-Watchdog Takes Powder" is included in the online *Anthology of World Poetry of the 20th Century, Vol. 10*: "Selected Contemporary American Poets," edited by Douglas Messerli (Green Integer/ Project for Innovative Poetry, 2016).

The author is grateful to the publishers/editors of all the above, and regrets any omissions.

OTHER TITLES FROM THE SONG CAVE:

1. *A Dark Dreambox of Another Kind* by **Alfred Starr Hamilton**
2. *My Enemies* by **Jane Gregory**
3. *Rude Woods* by **Nate Klug**
4. *Georges Braque and Others* by **Trevor Winkfield**
5. *The Living Method* by **Sara Nicholson**
6. *Splash State* by **Todd Colby**
7. *Essay Stanzas* by **Thomas Meyer**
8. *Illustrated Games of Patience* by **Ben Estes**
9. *Dark Green* by **Emily Hunt**
10. *Honest James* by **Christian Schlegel**
11. *M* by **Hannah Brooks-Motl**
12. *What the Lyric Is* by **Sara Nicholson**
13. *The Hermit* by **Lucy Ives**
14. *The Orchid Stories* by **Kenward Elmslie**
15. *Do Not Be a Gentleman When You Say Goodnight* by **Mitch Sisskind**
16. *HAIRDO* by **Rachel B. Glaser**
17. *Motor Maids across the Continent* by **Ron Padgett**
18. *Songs for Schizoid Siblings* by **Lionel Ziprin**
19. *Professionals of Hope*, The Selected Writings of **Subcomandante Marcos**
20. *Fort Not* by **Emily Skillings**
21. *Riddles, Etc.* by **Geoffrey Hilsabeck**

22. *CHARAS: The Improbable Dome Builders*, by **Syeus Mottel** (Co-published with Pioneer Works)
23. *YEAH NO* by **Jane Gregory**
24. *Nioque of the Early-Spring* by **Francis Ponge**
25. *Smudgy and Lossy* by **John Myers**
26. *The Desert* by **Brandon Shimoda**
27. *Scardanelli* by **Friederike Mayröcker**
28. *The Alley of Fireflies and other stories* by **Raymond Roussel**
29. *CHANGES: Notes on Choreography* by **Merce Cunningham** (Co-published with the Merce Cunningham Trust)
30. *My Mother Laughs* by **Chantal Akerman**
31. *Earth* by **Hannah Brooks-Motl**